Just Wanted to Say Hi

ELLYN SANNA

BARBOUR
PUBLISHING, INC.

Just Wanted to Say Hi

It's no special occasion. . .

I don't have anything particular to say. . .

But I'm thinking of you. . .

And I just wanted to say hi.

I'm thinking about you today, hoping that things are well with you and wishing you. . .

sunshine,
the enjoyment of simple pleasures,
a day filled with delight,
the knowledge of God's presence,
and wings to fly.

If I had a single flower

for every time I think about you

I could walk forever in my garden.

CLAUDIA GRANDI

1

Wishing You Sunshine

I hope today is bright for you. I'm praying that if any clouds fill your life today, you'll be able to see the sun break through. Don't worry about those clouds, and don't linger in the shadows. Focus on the sunshine. See how lovely the light is as it streams into your life. Allow it to illumine all the blessings God has given you.

Fix your thoughts on what is true and honorable and right.
Think about things that are excellent and worthy of praise. . .
and the God of peace will be with you.

PHILIPPIANS 4:8–9 NLT

Never lose an opportunity of seeing anything that is beautiful;
for beauty is God's handwriting—a wayside sacrament.
Welcome it in every fair face, in every fair sky,
in every fair flower, and thank God for it as a cup of blessing.

RALPH WALDO EMERSON

I will send down showers in season;
there will be showers of blessing.

EZEKIEL 34:26 NIV

The wonderful thing about sunset,
and much the same can be said for sunrise,
is that it happens every day,
and even if the sunset itself is not spectacular,
it marks the beginning of another day.
It's a great time to pause and take notice.

ELAINE ST. JAMES

May the rising and setting of the sun today make you pause and take notice of all that God had done in your life. Each new day that comes is blessed with promise; each day that passes is filled with holy gifts for you to look back and unwrap.

Just Wanted to Say Hi

I find each day too short for all the thoughts I want to think,
all the walks I want to take,
all the books I want to read,
and all the friends I want to see.
The longer I live,
the more my mind dwells upon the beauty
and the wonder of the world.

JOHN BURROUGHS

I hope times passes quickly for you, filled up with sunny thoughts and bright events. But I also pray your days go slowly enough that you find time for all that really matters. May your mind dwell on the world's beauty and wonder.

*Into all lives, in many simple, familiar, homely ways,
God infuses this element of joy from the surprises of life,
which unexpectedly brighten our days,
and fill our eyes with light.*

LONGFELLOW

May your life be full of

God's joyful surprises!

Write on your heart that every day is the best day of the year.

RALPH WALDO EMERSON

I know today is no special occasion—
but I suspect God wants every day to be a celebration.
Each day He comes to you with new blessings.
I hope you'll have time today to notice all those blessings—
and say thank You.

We may run, walk, stumble. . . , or fly,
but let us never lose sight of the reason for the journey,
or miss a chance to see a rainbow on the way.

GLORIA GAITHER

I know sometimes you feel too tired to rejoice, too busy to play, too overwhelmed to praise God. . .

But take a minute to walk in the sunshine. If the sun seems hidden behind the clouds, look for a rainbow, the promise of better times ahead.

And maybe—if no one's looking—instead of walking in the light, you could skip or even dance.

2

Wishing You
the Enjoyment of
Simple Pleasures

Try not to be so busy that you miss the many small gifts that God's offering you today. Take time to enjoy life. Each moment of life is a tiny treasure, filled with new blessings from the God who loves you.

What happens when we live God's way?
He brings gifts into our lives,
much the same way that fruit appears in an orchard....

GALATIANS 5:22 THE MESSAGE

16

Look to this day!

For it is life, the very life of life.

For yesterday is but a dream

And tomorrow is only a vision,

But today well lived makes every yesterday

a dream of happiness

And tomorrow a vision of hope.

Look well, therefore, to this day!

Such is the salutation of the dawn.

KALIDASA

I want to learn to live each moment
and be grateful for what it brings, asking no more.

GLORIA GAITHER

Attaining inner simplicity is learning to live
happily in the present moment.
Keep in mind that life is a continuous succession
of present moments.

ELAINE ST. JAMES

There are no little things.
"Little things," so called, are the hinges of the universe.

FANNY FERN

Nothing taken for granted;
everything received with gratitude;
everything passed on with grace.

G. K. CHESTERTON

Live today fully, expressing gratitude for all you have been,
all you are right now, and all you are becoming.

MELODIE BEATTIE

The best things are nearest:
breath in your nostrils, light in your eyes, flowers at your feet,
duties at your hand, the path of God just before you.

ROBERT LOUIS STEVENSON

*To be alive, to be able to see, to walk,
to have a home, . . .friends—it's all a miracle.
I have adopted the technique of living life
from miracle to miracle.*

ARTHUR RUBENSTEIN

Nay you step from one small miracle to the next
as you live your life today.

*Isn't everything you have and everything you are
sheer gifts from God?*

1 CORINTHIANS 4:7–8 THE MESSAGE

3

Wishing You a Day Filled with Delight

Just Wanted to Say Hi

See! The winter is past;
the rains are over and gone.
Flowers appear on the earth;
the season of singing has come.

SONG OF SOLOMON 2:11–12 NIV

It may be just an ordinary day today—but I'm
praying that your hours will be filled with delight.

Just Wanted to Say Hi

*If you surrender completely to the moments as they pass,
you live more richly those moments.*

ANNE MORROW LINDBERGH

Just to be is a blessing.

Just to live is holy.

ABRAHAM HESCHEL

*Life is what we are alive to. It is not length but breadth. . . .
Be alive to. . .goodness, kindness, purity, love, history,
poetry, music, flowers, stars, God, and eternal hope.*

MALTBIE D. BABCOCK

*I am beginning to learn that it is
the sweet, simple things of life which are the real ones after all.*

LAURA INGALLS WILDER

All along life's broad highway

I found loveliness today.

CARLETON EVERETT KNOX

*There is no event so commonplace
but that God is present within it. . .
always leaving you room to recognize Him
or not recognize Him. . . .*

FREDERICK BUECHNER

*Because of our routines we often forget that
life is an ongoing adventure.*

MAYA ANGELOU

*There are only two ways to live your life.
One is as though nothing is a miracle.
The other is as though everything is a miracle.*

ALBERT EINSTEIN

*Blue skies with white clouds on summer days.
A myriad of stars on clear moonlit nights.
Tulips and roses and violets and dandelions and daisies.
Bluebirds and laughter and sunshine and Easter.
See how He loves us!*

ALICE CHAPIN

Only the heart knows how to find what is precious.

FYODOR DOSTOYEVSKY

May you have heart—

eyes to see what is truly precious in your life.

It is only with the heart that one can see right.
What is essential is invisible to the eye.

ANTOINE DE SAINT-EXUPÉRY

4

Wishing You the Knowledge of God's Presence

Just Wanted to Say Hi

For God is sheer beauty,

all-generous in love, loyal always and ever.

PSALM 100:5 THE MESSAGE

Sometimes God's presence is so real that we get goose bumps of awe. But most of the time, as we live our humdrum lives, we're not aware that God is with us, as close as the air we breathe.

I'm praying that today, as you go about your routine, you'll sense God's quiet love in all you do, in all those you meet, and in every breath you take.

Each moment contains a hundred messages from God.
To each cry of "Oh, Lord," God answers, "I am here."

RUMI

May your heart today be right with God. . .

so that you can hear His voice.

You're blessed when you get your inside world—
your mind and heart—put right.
Then you can see God in the outside world.

MATTHEW 5:6 THE MESSAGE

29

I often think we must disappoint our kind Father
by not noticing the little things
(as well as the countless great things)
that He does to give us pleasure.

AMY CARMICHAEL

May you see the footprints of

the Holy in all the small details of your life.

God wants us to be present where we are.
He invites us to see and to hear what is around us and,
through it all, to discern the footprints of the Holy.

RICHARD J. FOSTER

To be glad of life,
because it gives you the chance to love
and to work and to play and to look up at the stars. . .
to think seldom of your enemies, often of your friends,
and every day of Christ, and to spend as much time as you can,
with body and spirit in God's out-of-doors—
these are little guideposts on the footpath of peace.

HENRY VAN DYKE

Look around today.

See God's guideposts everywhere!

Just Wanted to Say Hi

Reflection. . .enables our minds to be
stretched in three different directions—
the direction that leads to a proper relationship with God,
the relationship that leads to a healthy relationship with others,
and the relationship that leads to a
deeper understanding of oneself.

MARK CONNOLLY

Take time today for quiet moments of reflection.

Walk and talk and work and laugh with your friends,
but behind the scenes keep up the life of
simple prayer and inward worship.

THOMAS S. KELLY

5

Wishing You
Wings to Fly

Be like the bird that, halting in its flight
Awhile on boughs too slight,
Feels them give way beneath her, and yet sings
Knowing that she hath wings.

VICTOR HUGO

Sometimes life seems like a freefall—but today I'm praying that you'll trust God's wings to bear you up. He won't let you fall.

Just Wanted to Say Hi

Like an eagle that rouses her chicks

and hovers over her young,

so he spread his wings to them in

and carried them aloft on his pinions.

DEUTERONOMY 32:11 NLT

You can't try your wings if you're sitting on the nest.

LISA BEVERE

Don't be afraid to fly!

Ye have seen what I did. . .
and how I bare you on eagle's wings,
and brought you unto myself.

EXODUS 19:4 KJV

But those who wait upon the LORD will find new strength.
They will fly high on wings like eagles.

ISAIAH 40:31 NLT

When you come to the edge of all the light you have,
and you must take a step into the darkness of the unknown,
believe that one of two things will happen.
Either there will be something solid for you to stand on—
or you will be taught how to fly.

PATRICK OVERTON

We look at our burdens and heavy loads and shrink from them;
but as we lift them and bind them about our hearts,
they become wings; and on them we rise and soar toward God.

MRS. CHARLES E. COWMAN

Reach high, for stars lie hidden in your soul. Dream deep, for every dream precedes the goal.

PAMELA VAULL STARR

May you fly high enough to touch the stars.

*If I take the wings of the morning,
and dwell in the uttermost parts of the sea;
Even there shall thy hand lead me,
and thy right hand shall hold me.*

PSALM 139:9–10 KJV

Some days we plod through life, one slow step at a time, our eyes on the ground ahead. We're so preoccupied with our busy routines that we forget to look up at the sky. And we've totally forgotten that God gave our hearts wings to fly.

But God asks us rise up above the clouds and see the sun. . .
He wants us to enjoy all life's smallest pleasures. . .
He longs to shower us with delight. . .
And He yearns for us to know that He is
with us.

That's why He lifts us up on eagles' wings—so we can see life from eternity's perspective.

Just Wanted to Say Hi

God greets us each day with love. "Hello," He whispers to our hearts. "I love you."

Today, I'm adding my voice to His to tell you I'm thinking of you.

I just wanted to say hi, and let you know my prayer for you:

May the Lord continually bless you

with heaven's blessings

as well as with human joys.

PSALM 128:5 TLB